Contents

How to use this book

Each page has a title telling you what it is about.

Instructions look like this. Always read these carefully before starting.

This is Owl. Ask your teacher if you need to do his questions.

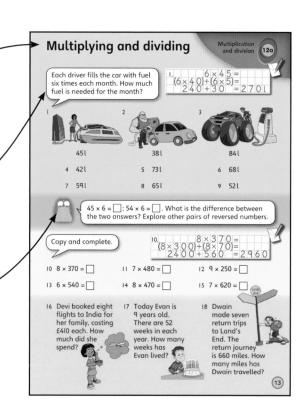

This shows you how to set out your work. The first question is done for you.

Read these word problems very carefully. Decide how you will work out the answers.

These are exploratory activities. You may like to do them with a partner.

Multiplying and dividing

Multiply each number by 10.

1. $378 \times 10 = 3780$

1	378	2	251	3	975	4	628
5	486	6	563	7	374	8	652
9	100	10	58	11	191	12	763

Now multiply each number by 100.

Look at each safe. Find one-tenth of the money.

13. $£120 \div 10 = £12$

13

£120

14

£240

15

£360

16

£7540

17

£560

18

£4740

19

£8320

20
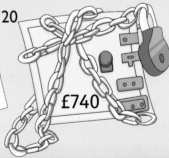
£740

You have £10. Multiply it by 10. Keep going. How many times must you multiply by 10 to reach £1 000 000?

Multiplying and dividing

Multiply each number by 10 and choose the correct answer. 1. (c)

1 4760
   (a) 4760
   (b) 4706
   (c) 47600

2 5111
   (a) 51101
   (b) 50111
   (c) 51110

3 3182
   (a) 31802
   (b) 31820
   (c) 30180

4 6556
   (a) 60556
   (b) 65506
   (c) 65560

5 109
   (a) 1090
   (b) 1099
   (c) 1990

6 4000
   (a) 40000
   (b) 400
   (c) 4004

7 250
   (a) 255
   (b) 2500
   (c) 25000

8 9910
   (a) 9919
   (b) 990
   (c) 99100

Divide each number by 10.

9. $6200 \div 10 = 620$

9 6200

10 7800

11 8400

12 3600

13 2800

14 5700

15 1900

16 8600

17 3900

18 4400

19 9600

20 5300

Divide each number by 100.

 Start with 1000. Work with a partner. One person multiplies by 10, the other divides by 10. Spin a coin to decide who operates on the number. Try to reach either 1 or 1 million.

Multiplying and dividing

Copy and complete.

1. $380 \times 10 = 3800$

1 $380 \times 10 = \square$	2 $46 \div 10 = \square$	3 $101 \times 10 = \square$
4 $535 \div 10 = \square$	5 $624 \div 10 = \square$	6 $425 \times 10 = \square$
7 $237 \times 100 = \square$	8 $760 \div 100 = \square$	9 $65 \times 100 = \square$

Buy 10 of each.

10. $£1 \cdot 60 \times 10 = £16 \cdot 00$

10
£1·60

11
£2·70

12
£3·40

13
£4·50

14
£3·90

15
£2·60

16
£1·20

17
£4·20

18 Hasib had 48 meal worms. His Dad said that within 1 month he would have ten times this number. After 1 month he had 390 meal worms. How far was his Dad wrong?

19 A goalkeeper won £700. He bought a suit for £218 and split the rest between his ten team mates. How much did he give each team mate?

20 The temperature at Christmas is 3·4°C. If it is ten times this on a midsummer day, what is the temperature?

Write a word problem with the answer 42 using either multiplying or dividing by 10. Give it to your partner to answer.

Multiplying and dividing

Divide each score by 100.

1 270

2 340

3 510

4 5700

5 620

6 8400

7 490

8 6300

9 920

Write the final scores in order, smallest to largest.

10 Multiply each star number by each circle number.

10. $60 \times 200 = 12,000$

60

200

40

800

20

700

90

Two different multiples of 100 have a product of 720 000. What could they be?

Rounding

Round each number to the nearest 100. Use the number line to help you.

1. 6324 → 6300

300 6310 6320 6330 6340 6350 6360 6370 6380 6390 6400

| 1 6324 | 2 6384 | 3 6378 | 4 6321 | 5 6350 |
| 6 6349 | 7 6399 | 8 6333 | 9 6301 | 10 6355 |

Round each number to the nearest 1000.

11. 4268 → 4000

000 5000 6000

| 11 4268 | 12 5821 | 13 4932 | 14 5007 | 15 5199 |
| 16 4419 | 17 5376 | 18 5757 | 19 4279 | 20 4635 |

Round each number to the nearest 10.

21. 1656 → 1660

1650 1660 1670

| 21 1656 | 22 1667 | 23 1652 | 24 1669 | 25 1664 |
| 26 1653 | 27 1662 | 28 1665 | 29 1654 | 30 1658 |

Write two numbers that round to 3000 as the nearest 1000. Both numbers must have different digits. Are your numbers the same as your partner's?

Rounding

Round each number to the nearest 100. Use the number line to help you.

1. 5983 → 6000

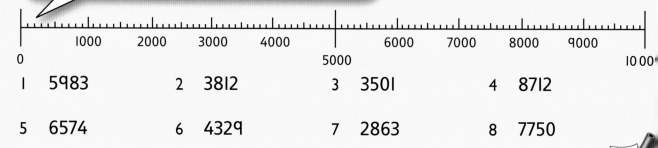

| 1000 | 2000 | 3000 | 4000 | | 6000 | 7000 | 8000 | 9000 |
0   5000   10 000

| 1 | 5983 | 2 | 3812 | 3 | 3501 | 4 | 8712 |

| 5 | 6574 | 6 | 4329 | 7 | 2863 | 8 | 7750 |

Round each amount to the nearest £100.

9. £468 → £500

9  £468

10 £3750

11 £16 458

12 £271

13 £28 650

14  £5127

15 £6833

16 £724

17 Basanti's father said that whatever she saved by her birthday, he would give her the same amount rounded to the nearest £100. She has already saved £270. How much more must she save to get £400 from him?

18 Gemma can take her baggage on the plane as long as it weighs 20 kg or less, rounded to the nearest 1 kg. What is the heaviest suitcase she can take?

Write your own word problem involving rounding to the nearest 100.

Rounding

Round each distance to the nearest (a) 1000, (b) 100 and (c) 10 miles or km.

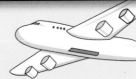

```
1. 1 2,3 8 5
   (a) 1 2,0 0 0 miles
   (b) ...
```

1 Sydney 12 385 miles

2 Cape Town 4872 km

3 Mexico City 13 672 km

4 Gibraltar 6502 miles

5 Hong Kong 14 038 miles

6 Cairo 2181 miles

7 New York 11 737 km

8 Athens 4392 km

Estimate each product by rounding both numbers.

```
9. 7 8 2 × 4 3 =
   8 0 0 × 4 0 = 3 2,0 0 0
```

9 782 × 43

10 223 × 68

11 531 × 57

12 874 × 21

13 467 × 33

14 626 × 78

15 920 × 56

16 187 × 23

17 579 × 41

🔍 **Explore**

Write a number that will round to the same number when rounded to the nearest 1000, 100 and 10.

Can you write another?

How many numbers like this are there between 5000 and 6000?

Rounding

Each dog collects the newspaper every day except Christmas Day, Boxing Day and Easter Sunday. Approximately how far does each dog run in a year?

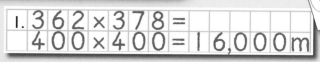

1. $362 \times 378 = $
$400 \times 400 = 16,000$ m

1   runs 378 m

2   runs 749 m

3   runs 911 m

4   runs 560 m

5   runs 310 m

6   runs 105 m

7   runs 468 m

8   runs 208 m

9   runs 844 m

True or false?

10   The number of days in a decade rounds to the number 3000.

11   If a number rounds up to the nearest thousand, it must round up to the nearest hundred.

12   If a number has a 9 as its last digit, it can never be rounded down.

13   It is possible for a number to round to zero.

14   The number 999 500 rounds to one million as its nearest thousand.

Write a number that rounds **up** to the nearest 1000; **down** to the nearest 100; **up** to the nearest 10. Find other numbers like this.

Multiplying and dividing

How much pocket money does each child receive?

1. $4 \times 6p = 24p$
    $4 \times 60p = 240p$
    $= £2 \cdot 40$

1
60p per week for 4 weeks

2
70p per week for 6 weeks

3
30p per week for 9 weeks

4
80p per week for 4 weeks

5
50p per week for 5 weeks

6
40p per week for 7 weeks

7
30p per week for 5 weeks

8
40p per week for 6 weeks

9
50p per week for 7 weeks

Each worker works 5 days. How much does each earn?

10
£45 per day

11
£35 per day

10. $5 \times £45 = ...$

12
£55 per day

13
£25 per day

14
£65 per day

 Write a pair of numbers to make $\square \times \square\square = 360$.

11

Multiplying and dividing

How many grams does each kitten eat in 1 week?

I.
$$7 \times 35 =$$
$$(7 \times 30) + (7 \times 5) =$$
$$210 + 35 = 245g$$

1

35 g per day

2

64 g per day

3

54 g per day

4

28 g per day

5

37 g per day

6

65 g per day

7

49 g per day

8

36 g per day

9
23 g per day

Copy and complete.

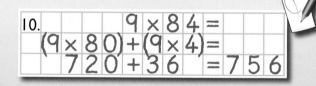

10.
$$9 \times 84 =$$
$$(9 \times 80) + (9 \times 4) =$$
$$720 + 36 = 756$$

10 $9 \times 84 = \boxed{}$

11 $4 \times 92 = \boxed{}$

12 $5 \times 75 = \boxed{}$

13 $6 \times 63 = \boxed{}$

14 $3 \times 58 = \boxed{}$

15 $2 \times 94 = \boxed{}$

16 $8 \times 76 = \boxed{}$

17 $7 \times 46 = \boxed{}$

18 $6 \times 69 = \boxed{}$

Write three different pairs of numbers to make $\boxed{} \times \boxed{} \boxed{} = 252$.

Multiplying and dividing

Each driver fills the car with fuel six times each month. How much fuel is needed for the month?

1.
$$6 \times 45 =$$
$$(6 \times 40) + (6 \times 5) =$$
$$240 + 30 = 270\,l$$

1   45 l

2   38 l

3   84 l

4   42 l

5   73 l

6   68 l

7   59 l

8   65 l

9   52 l

$45 \times 6 = \square$; $54 \times 6 = \square$. What is the difference between the two answers? Explore other pairs of reversed numbers.

Copy and complete.

10.
$$8 \times 370 =$$
$$(8 \times 300) + (8 \times 70) =$$
$$2400 + 560 = 2960$$

10 $8 \times 370 = \square$

11 $7 \times 480 = \square$

12 $9 \times 250 = \square$

13 $6 \times 540 = \square$

14 $8 \times 470 = \square$

15 $7 \times 620 = \square$

16 Devi booked eight flights to India for her family, costing £410 each. How much did she spend?

17 Today Evan is 9 years old. There are 52 weeks in each year. How many weeks has Evan lived?

18 Dwain made seven return trips to Land's End. The return journey is 660 miles. How many miles has Dwain travelled?

13

Multiplying and dividing

 How much flour has been ground each time?

1.
$$3 \times 480 =$$
$$(3 \times 400) + (3 \times 80) =$$
$$1200 + 240 = 1440g$$

 1
480 g
3 bags

2
370 g
7 bags

3
240 g
8 bags

4
530 g
7 bags

5
320 g
4 bags

6
610 g
6 bags

7
430 g
5 bags

8
590 g
8 bags

Rachel orders 2 kg of flour. Look at the bags above. Which total is closest to her order?

True or false?

9 45 × 9 is 90 more than 7 × 45.

10 5 × 560 is 200 less than 3000.

11 3 × 980 is less than 5 × 860.

12 10 000 is double the product of 5 and 750.

13 50 × 30 is double 25 × 60.

14 7 × 500 is the same as 50 × 7 × 10.

Multiplying and dividing

Copy and complete.

1   $6 \times 25 =$ ☐

2   $8 \times 25 =$ ☐

3   $7 \times 25 =$ ☐

4   $11 \times 25 =$ ☐

5   $20 \times 25 =$ ☐

6   $25 \times 9 =$ ☐

7   $25 \times 30 =$ ☐

8   $25 \times 33 =$ ☐

9   $25 \times 28 =$ ☐

10 $25 \times 42 =$ ☐

11 $51 \times 25 =$ ☐

12 $25 \times 19 =$ ☐

Each episode of Space Adventure is 25 minutes long. For each boxed set, write the total time in minutes.

13.
	3	2	×	1	0	0	=	3	2	0	0	
									1	6	0	0	
	3	2	×	2	5		=	8	0	0		minutes

13

32 episodes

14

28 episodes

15

45 episodes

16

56 episodes

17

35 episodes

18

42 episodes

🔍 Explore

Can you find a quick way of multiplying by 75?

Use these facts to help you:

$300 \div 3 = 100$ Double 75 is 150 $4 \times 75 = 300$

Try different ways. Discuss your preferred method with your partner.

Multiplying and dividing

Each cyclist makes 14 journeys. How many miles does each cyclist ride?

1.
$$7 \times 35 = (7 \times 30) + (7 \times 5)$$
$$= 210 + 35$$
$$= 245$$
$$14 \times 35 = 490 \text{ miles}$$

1

35 miles

2

48 miles

3

27 miles

4

52 miles

5

38 miles

6

45 miles

7   64 miles   8   23 miles   9   57 miles

10 71 miles   11 44 miles   12 31 miles

Complete these calculations by halving and doubling.

13.
$$26 \times 6 = (20 \times 6) + (6 \times 6)$$
$$= 120 + 36$$
$$= 156$$
$$26 \times 12 = 312$$

13 26 × 12   14 37 × 16   15 54 × 18   16 45 × 14

17 62 × 16   18 17 × 14   19 28 × 24   20 23 × 22

The area of this square is 11 × 11 = 121 cm². Find areas of the following squares: 12 × 12, 15 × 15, 16 × 16.

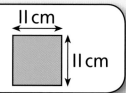

11 cm

11 cm

Complete these multiplications by doubling one number and halving the other.

$$1. \; 12 \times 53 = 6 \times 106$$
$$= 600 + 36$$
$$= 636$$

1 12 × 53 = ☐

2 14 × 42 = ☐

3 18 × 21 = ☐

4 16 × 34 = ☐

5 23 × 14 = ☐

6 37 × 12 = ☐

7 32 × 18 = ☐

8 27 × 36 = ☐

9 45 × 16 = ☐

10 Josh bought 6 football stickers every week. How many stickers did he have after exactly 1 year?
After 2 years?
After 3 years?

11 Gayatri earned £25 for each car she cleaned. How much did she earn for cleaning 23 cars? How many more cars must she clean to earn £700?

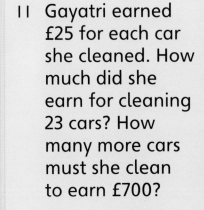

12 Paul scored 288 points on his video game. Anil scored 8 times his score and Tom scored $\frac{1}{4}$ of Anil's score. Write their scores.

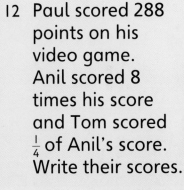

There are 8 packets of crisps in a value pack. How many packets?

$$13. \; 26 \rightarrow 52 \rightarrow 104 \rightarrow 208$$
$$26 \times 8 = 208$$

13 26 packs

14 36 packs

15 42 packs

16 55 packs

17 48 packs

18 52 packs

 Work with a partner. Together work out how many months old you are. How about others in your families?

Multiplying and dividing

Copy and complete.

1. 2 4 8 → 1 2 4 → 6 2 → 3 1
   2 4 8 ÷ 8 = 3 1

1   248 ÷ 8 =

2   360 ÷ 8 =

3   216 ÷ 8 =

4   272 ÷ 8 =

5   96 ÷ 8 =

6   1024 ÷ 8 =

7   120 ÷ 8 =

8   2848 ÷ 8 =

9   168 ÷ 8 =

Explore

Try to find a quick way of creating the 32 times table using doubling.

Are there other big tables you can find?

Find the missing numbers.

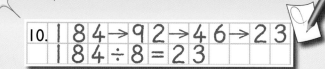

10. 1 8 4 → 9 2 → 4 6 → 2 3
    1 8 4 ÷ 8 = 2 3

10 8 × ⭐ = 184

11 ⭐ × 16 = 208

12 29 × 8 = ⭐

13 25 × ⭐ = 400

14 16 × ⭐ = 512

15 26 × 16 = ⭐

16 ⭐ × 8 = 280

17 32 × ⭐ = 512

What is one-eighth of £1 000 000? Discuss with a partner.

18

Multiplying

1   Copy and complete this multiplication table.

×	40	200	60	700	90	300
5	200					
7						
3						
8						

Investigate what multiplications will have an answer of 2400.

Copy and complete.

2.	200	70	5		6 0 0
3	600	210	15	+	2 1 0
					1 5
					8 2 5

$275 \times 3 = 825$

2   200 70 5

3 □□□

$275 \times 3 =$ ⭐

3   300 40 2

4 □□□

$342 \times 4 =$ ⭐

4   400 20 3

5 □□□

$423 \times 5 =$ ⭐

5   $158 \times 6 =$ ⭐

6   $439 \times 5 =$ ⭐

7   $618 \times 2 =$ ⭐

8   $264 \times 4 =$ ⭐

9   $397 \times 4 =$ ⭐

10   $561 \times 3 =$ ⭐

11   $482 \times 6 =$ ⭐

12   $279 \times 5 =$ ⭐

13   $845 \times 2 =$ ⭐

14   $659 \times 4 =$ ⭐

15   $354 \times 3 =$ ⭐

16   $415 \times 6 =$ ⭐

Write an estimate by rounding each 3-digit number to the nearest 100. Complete the multiplications.

1 $3 \times 146 = (3 \times 100) + (3 \times 40) + (3 \times 6) = 300 + 120 + 18 = \square$

2 $5 \times 243 = (5 \times 200) + (5 \times 40) + (5 \times 3) = \square$

3 $4 \times 317 = (4 \times \square) + (4 \times \square) + (4 \times \square) =$

4 $6 \times 128 = (6 \times \square) + (6 \times \square) + (6 \times \square) =$

Copy and complete.

5. $3 \times 4\,1\,6 = (3 \times 4\,0\,0)$

5 $416 \times 3 =$ 6 $279 \times 5 =$ 7 $186 \times 7 =$

8 $304 \times 6 =$ 9 $512 \times 4 =$ 10 $484 \times 3 =$

11 $879 \times 2 =$ 12 $618 \times 3 =$ 13 $376 \times 4 =$

These are the sales for one Saturday at the Electronics Superstore. Write the amount collected.

14 £274

sold 6

15 £187

sold 3

16 £368

sold 4

17 £126

sold 8

18 £434

sold 7

19 £835

sold 5

How many of each item can you buy for £2000?

Multiplying

Copy and complete these multiplications. Write your estimate first.

1 ⟨900⟩
   314
   ×   3
   ─────
            3 × 300
            3 × 10
            3 × 4
   ─────
   ─────

2 ⟨800⟩
   186
   ×   4
   ─────
            4 × 100
            4 × 80
            4 × 6
   ─────
   ─────

1. ⟨900⟩
   314
   ×   3
   ─────
   900   3 × 300
    30   3 × 10
    12   3 × 4
   ─────
   942

3   786 × 2   4   274 × 5   5   327 × 6   6   643 × 6

7   512 × 3   8   487 × 4   9   356 × 2   10 274 × 4

11 563 × 2   12 623 × 2   13 335 × 6   14 422 × 3

Find the cost of these holidays for (a) 4 people, (b) 5 people, (c) 7 people.

15

£346 each

16

£543 each

17

FRANCE

£236 each

18

£318 each

19

£274 each

20

£437 each

Either ☐☐ × ☐ or ☐☐☐ × ☐ = 648.
What numbers could make these work (for example 324 × 2)?

21

Multiplying

Estimate first, then complete the multiplications.

```
  1. 9 0 0
       2 7 6
   ×       3
     8 2 8
       2 1
```

1 276 × 3	2 436 × 4	3 147 × 6	4 382 × 6
5 247 × 5	6 523 × 3	7 193 × 6	8 318 × 7
9 274 × 8	10 356 × 6	11 412 × 5	12 564 × 3

13 What is the difference between the cost of 3 season tickets at £425 each for City and 4 season tickets at £316 each for Rovers?

14 Jason has won a prize. He can choose between £178 each month for 6 months or £235 each month for 4 months. Which should he choose to get the most money?

Explore

Use the digit cards

 3   4   5   6

Make a 3-digit number and a 1-digit number, and multiply them together.

What is the largest answer?

What is the smallest answer?

How many different answers can you make between 2000 and 3000?

Multiplying

Copy and complete.

$$1. \ 23 \times 20 = 23 \times 2 \times 10$$
$$= 46 \times 10$$
$$= 460$$

1 $23 \times 20 = \boxed{}$ 2 $33 \times 30 = \boxed{}$ 3 $41 \times 20 = \boxed{}$ 4 $16 \times 40 = \boxed{}$

5 $17 \times 50 = \boxed{}$ 6 $30 \times 14 = \boxed{}$ 7 $40 \times 18 = \boxed{}$ 8 $50 \times 21 = \boxed{}$

9 $70 \times 32 = \boxed{}$ 10 $60 \times 21 = \boxed{}$ 11 $33 \times 40 = \boxed{}$ 12 $20 \times 67 = \boxed{}$

Schools are buying new supplies for the new term. Write the cost of each.

$$13. \ 43 \times 20 = 43 \times 2 \times 10$$
$$= 86 \times 10$$
$$= 860 = £8·60$$

13

20p

43 pencils

14

30p

18 rulers

15
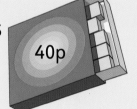
40p

24 rubbers

16

50p

17 pens

17

40p

23 crayons

18
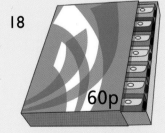
60p

34 sharpeners

How many boxes do you need to have 1000 pencils if they are packed in boxes of 20? How about boxes of 30? 40? 50?

Write an estimate by rounding each number to the nearest 10.

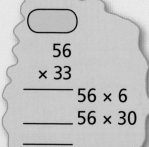

I. $20 \times 30 = 600$

1   $23 \times 31 = \square$ 2 $42 \times 29 = \square$ 3 $38 \times 22 = \square$ 4 $47 \times 18 = \square$

Copy and complete. Write your estimate first.

5
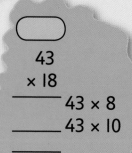
```
    43
  × 18
  ─────
        43 × 8
        43 × 10
  ─────
```

6
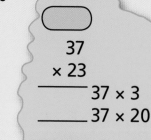
```
    37
  × 23
  ─────
        37 × 3
        37 × 20
  ─────
```

7
```
    56
  × 33
  ─────
        56 × 6
        56 × 30
  ─────
```

8   $\begin{array}{r} 53 \\ \times\ 16 \\ \hline \end{array}$

9   $\begin{array}{r} 47 \\ \times\ 22 \\ \hline \end{array}$

10   $\begin{array}{r} 39 \\ \times\ 33 \\ \hline \end{array}$

11   $\begin{array}{r} 52 \\ \times\ 19 \\ \hline \end{array}$

12   Amy has 1000 sweets. She gives 24 sweets to each child in her class. There are 31 children. How many sweets are left?

13   Janine is 34 years old. How many more weeks until she has lived for 2000 weeks?

14   Craig has 48 pieces of pipe, each 36 cm long. He joins them together. How long is the pipeline? How much longer to reach 20 m?

Write your own word problem using multiplication of 2-digit numbers.

Multiplying

Write how much the coach company will receive on each trip.

1.
```
    900
     32
  × 27
    224     32 × 7
    640     32 × 20
  £864
```

1 Mystery tour £32

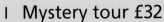

27 people

2 Sea and sand £42

18 people

3 Lakes and mountains £56

33 people

4 Famous gardens £33

32 people

5 City of London £63

41 people

6 Ancient castles £29

24 people

7 National parks £28

38 people

8 Birdwatching £42

26 people

9 Theme park £34

54 people

True or false?

10 38 × 23 = 23 × 38

11 41 × 25 = (41 × 20) + (41 × 5)

12 26 × 30 < 36 × 20

13 36 × 27 > 37 × 26

14 18 × 24 = 14 × 28

15 19 × 72 < 70 × 21

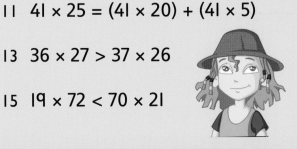

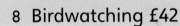

25

Multiplying

Complete these multiplications. Estimate first!

1. $\widehat{(1500)}$
   46
   ×27
   . . .

1	46 × 27	2	28 × 34	3	56 × 29	4	52 × 43

5	28 × 37	6	53 × 17	7	64 × 27	8	63 × 32

Write the area of these courts.

9

26 m

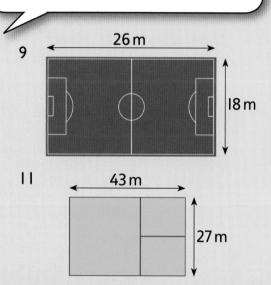

18 m

10

35 m

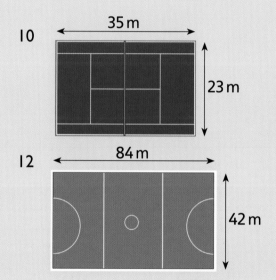

23 m

11

43 m

27 m

12

84 m

42 m

Explore

Use these place value cards to make two 2-digit numbers.

2 0	3 0	4 0	3	4	7

Multiply them together.

What are all the different possible answers?

Which is the largest? Which is the smallest?

Finding fractions of amounts

What fraction of the total cost does each person pay? Write the amount.

1. $\frac{1}{2}$ of £46 = £23

1 Manchester £46

2 Hull £63

3 Nottingham £55

4 Leeds £28

5 Lincoln £39

6 Leicester £70

7 York £66

8 Grimsby £48

9 Newcastle £25

 The trip to Bournemouth is £72. Write the cost for 2 people, 3 people, 4 people…

Copy and complete.

10. $\frac{1}{3}$ of 21 kg = 7 kg,
$\frac{2}{3}$ of 21 kg = 14 kg

10 $\frac{1}{3}$ of 21 kg = ☐, $\frac{2}{3}$ of 21 kg = ☐

11 $\frac{1}{5}$ of 45 kg = ☐, $\frac{3}{5}$ of 45 kg = ☐

12 $\frac{1}{4}$ of 36 kg = ☐, $\frac{3}{4}$ of 36 kg = ☐

13 $\frac{1}{6}$ of 42 kg = ☐, $\frac{5}{6}$ of 42 kg = ☐

14 $\frac{1}{8}$ of 48 kg = ☐, $\frac{5}{8}$ of 48 kg = ☐

27

Finding fractions of amounts

Write how much each child has saved.

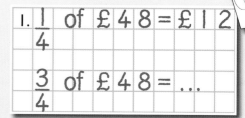

1. $\frac{1}{4}$ of £48 = £12

$\frac{3}{4}$ of £48 = ...

STRIKE!

1 Target £48   saved $\frac{3}{4}$

2 Target £27   saved $\frac{2}{3}$

3 Target £45   saved $\frac{2}{5}$

4 Target £60   saved $\frac{3}{10}$

5 Target £30   saved $\frac{4}{5}$

6 Target £24   saved $\frac{3}{8}$

7 Target £30   saved $\frac{5}{6}$

8 Target £28   saved $\frac{4}{7}$

9 Target £45   saved $\frac{7}{9}$

You need £60 to reach a target. What fraction could you have saved, and what could your target be? For example, you could have saved $\frac{1}{2}$ of a target of £120.

Copy and complete.

10. $\frac{1}{5}$ of £25 = £5, $\frac{3}{5}$ of £25 = £15

10 $\frac{3}{5}$ of £25 = ☐

11 $\frac{2}{3}$ of 21 cm = ☐

12 $\frac{7}{10}$ of 80 g = ☐

13 $\frac{3}{4}$ of 12 km = ☐

14 $\frac{5}{6}$ of 300 ml = ☐

15 $\frac{7}{9}$ of 18 m = ☐

16 $\frac{3}{8}$ of 40 l = ☐

17 $\frac{2}{7}$ of 63 kg = ☐

18 $\frac{4}{6}$ of 18 g = ☐

19 $\frac{2}{3}$ of 24 cm = ☐

20 $\frac{5}{7}$ of 63 l = ☐

21 $\frac{3}{4}$ of 48 m = ☐

22 $\frac{4}{5}$ of 60 kg = ☐

23 $\frac{2}{6}$ of 300 ml = ☐

24 $\frac{5}{6}$ of 360 m = ☐

Finding fractions of amounts

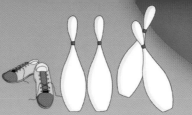

Find $\frac{1}{4}$ of each by halving, then halving again.

1. $\frac{1}{2}$ of $48 = 24$, $\frac{1}{4}$ of $48 = 12$

| 1 | 48 | 2 | 136 | 3 | 248 | 4 | 1024 |

STRIKE!

Find $\frac{1}{8}$ of each by halving, halving again, then halving again.

| 5 | 184 | 6 | 104 | 7 | 152 | 8 | 232 |

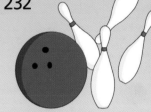

Find $\frac{1}{6}$ of each by halving, then dividing by 3.

| 9 | 126 | 10 | 186 | 11 | 138 | 12 | 348 |

Use halving to find these fractions.

13 $\frac{3}{4}$ of 128 14 $\frac{5}{8}$ of 336 15 $\frac{3}{8}$ of 328

16 $\frac{3}{4}$ of 420 17 $\frac{5}{6}$ of 126 18 $\frac{7}{8}$ of 184

13. $\frac{1}{2}$ of $128 = 64$

$\frac{1}{4}$ of $128 = 32$

$\frac{3}{4}$ of $128 = 96$

19 The lottery jackpot was £1200. James had 3 of the 8 winning tickets. How much did he win?

20 5 out of every 6 children don't like spiders. In a school of 282 children, how many don't like spiders?

21 Would you prefer to have $\frac{3}{5}$ of £45 or $\frac{4}{9}$ of £63?

Finding fractions of amounts

Which is the largest, and which is the smallest?

1 (a) $\frac{1}{2}$ of 24   (b) $\frac{1}{3}$ of 30   (c) $\frac{1}{4}$ of 32   (d) $\frac{1}{5}$ of 45

2 (a) $\frac{2}{3}$ of 39   (b) $\frac{3}{4}$ of 44   (c) $\frac{2}{5}$ of 80   (d) $\frac{3}{7}$ of 56

3 (a) $\frac{4}{5}$ of 135   (b) $\frac{6}{7}$ of 126   (c) $\frac{7}{10}$ of 270   (d) $\frac{3}{8}$ of 144

4 (a) $\frac{5}{9}$ of 630   (b) $\frac{3}{5}$ of 750   (c) $\frac{7}{8}$ of 560   (d) $\frac{6}{11}$ of 880

5 (a) $\frac{7}{100}$ of 800   (b) $\frac{9}{10}$ of 90   (c) $\frac{11}{20}$ of 120   (d) $\frac{4}{5}$ of 200

Write each set in order, smallest to largest.

Find the missing numbers.

6 $\frac{\square}{8}$ of 16 = 6   7 $\frac{\square}{3}$ of 21 = 14   8 $\frac{\square}{5}$ of 100 = 60

9 $\frac{\square}{8}$ of 56 = 49   10 $\frac{\square}{6}$ of 48 = 40   11 $\frac{\square}{9}$ of 45 = 25

 Explore

Here are three ways of making 36: $\frac{3}{4}$ of 48 $\frac{2}{3}$ of 54 $\frac{4}{5}$ of 45

Investigate how many different ways like this you can find for 24.

Hint: the numerators of the fractions must divide exactly into 24.

Now try to find different ways of making 72.

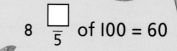

Tenths and hundredths

Write the fraction coloured in each large square. Write each as a decimal.

1. $\dfrac{35}{100} = 0.35$

1

2
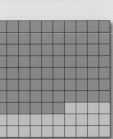
3

4
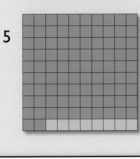
5

6

Now write the fraction that is not shaded each time.

$\dfrac{1}{4}$ = 25 hundredths. Explore other fractions that can be written as hundredths.

Copy and complete.

7. 37 hundredths = $\dfrac{3}{10} + \dfrac{7}{100}$

7 37 hundredths = $\dfrac{\square}{10} + \dfrac{7}{100}$

8 $\dfrac{46}{100}$ = ☐ tenths + ☐ hundredths

9 $2\dfrac{64}{100} = 2 + \dfrac{\square}{10} + \dfrac{\square}{100}$

10 74 hundredths = $\dfrac{\square}{10} + \dfrac{\square}{100}$

11 $4\dfrac{32}{100} = 4 + \dfrac{\square}{10} + \dfrac{\square}{100}$

12 $\dfrac{53}{100}$ = ☐ tenths + ☐ hundredths

13 $3\dfrac{14}{100} = 3 + \dfrac{\square}{10} + \dfrac{\square}{100}$

Tenths and hundredths

Write the value of the highlighted digit.

1.4 units

1 4·32	2 5·16	3 7·8	4 2·04
5 17·38	6 26·41	7 8·30	8 34·17
9 2·39	10 4·18	11 27	12 0·06
13 6·42	14 93	15 12·7	16 7·06

True or false?

17   $0·6 = 0·60$

18   $0·73 = 0·7 + 0·03$

19   $0·64 > 0·8$

20   $0·5 < 0·37$

21   $2\frac{37}{100} < 2·4$

22   $1·6 > 1\frac{57}{100}$

Write each set in order, smallest to largest.

23
9·14   8·76   9·05
8·71   9·41   8·9

24
£35   £35·23   £35·60
£36   £35·75   £35·57

25
2·53   2·35   2·05
2·50   2·0   2·30

26
£44·10   £43·90   £44·07
£43·97   £44   £44·50

27
6·97   7   7·04
7·23   7·1   6·9

28
0·07   0·4   0·12
0·46   0·5   0·09

Write eight different decimal numbers between 3 and 5 whose digits have a total of 12, e.g. 4·35. Put them in order, smallest first.

Tenths and hundredths

1   Write the position of each pointer.

1. (a) 2·15

2   Claire's luggage weighs 4·49 kg and Salim's is 4·68 kg. The limit is 4·5 kg. Whose luggage is over the limit, and by how much?

3   Side A of a picture measures 13·17 cm. Side B is 13·13 cm. Which side is longer? What is the perimeter of the picture?

Write each weight.

4   3   kg   4

5   4   kg   6

6   3·4   kg   3·5

7   10   kg   12

8   0·9   kg   1·1

9   5·7   kg   5·9

How many numbers with tenths and hundredths are there between $3\frac{1}{2}$ and $3\frac{3}{4}$?

Tenths and hundredths

Name	Running time (s)	Swimming time (s)	Cycling time (s)
Sufia	12·34	39·48	27·4
Chang	12·4	40·25	27·03
Emma	12·37	39·9	28·2
Josh	12·45	40·1	28·05
Vijay	12·03	40·06	27·2
Scott	12·33	39·55	28·47
Kim	12·35	40·03	27·53

In each race, who:

1. Running: Vijay,...

1   won?

2   came third?

3   came fifth?

4   came last?

5   came just after Emma?

6   came just before Josh?

7   What is the time difference between the first and last in each race?

8   In the three races, who had the shortest overall time?

Write a number between:

9   5·6 and 6·5

10   4·32 and 4·35

11   4·7 and 4·8

12   4·65 and 4·6

13   4·7 and 4·72

14   5 and 4·96

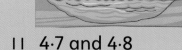

Explore

Use one of each of these digit cards: [4] [7] [0] [6]

Make decimal numbers, either ☐.☐ or ☐.☐☐ .

Investigate how many numbers you can make between 5 and 8.
Put them in order.

Coordinates

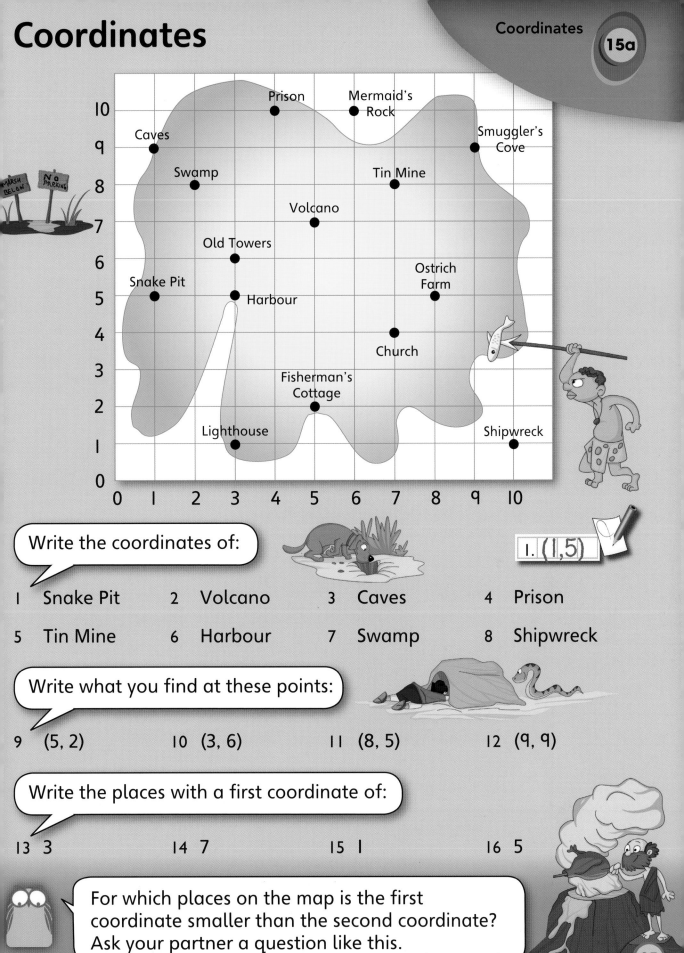

Write the coordinates of:

1. (1,5)

1　Snake Pit　　2　Volcano　　3　Caves　　4　Prison

5　Tin Mine　　6　Harbour　　7　Swamp　　8　Shipwreck

Write what you find at these points:

9　(5, 2)　　10　(3, 6)　　11　(8, 5)　　12　(9, 9)

Write the places with a first coordinate of:

13　3　　14　7　　15　1　　16　5

For which places on the map is the first
coordinate smaller than the second coordinate?
Ask your partner a question like this.

35

Coordinates

Write the coordinates of:

1. (4,5)

1 Forton   2 Elmbridge

Write the horizontal coordinate of:

3 Carby   4 Gorle

5 Danton   6 Arndale

Write the vertical coordinate of:

7 Hoke   8 Bigby   9 Tayford   10 Shorton

11 Write the places where the horizontal coordinate is 4.

12 Write the places where the vertical coordinate is 6.

Write the place you reach if you start at:

13 (2, 5), go East two squares   14 (7, 4), go North three squares

15 (4, 3), go West three squares, North three squares

16 (5, 7), go South five squares, West 3 squares

17 (0, 2), go North-East four squares, South one square

18 (3, 0), go North-West two squares, North six squares, South-East three squares

You can only move along gridlines. Each space is 1 km. How many different places could you visit if you didn't want to go further than 12 km?

Coordinates

Write the coordinates of the vertices of each shape.

1. (2, 1), (. .), (. .)

1
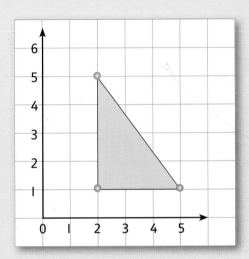

2
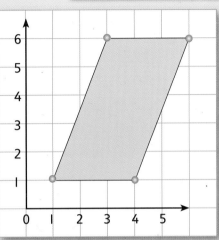

Draw 8 × 8 coordinate grids on squared paper. Plot the points and join them to make a shape. Write the name of the shape.

3   (3, 5), (7, 5), (5, 2)   4   (2, 3), (2, 6), (6, 3), (6, 6)

5   (0, 2), (0, 8), (2, 4), (6, 4)   6   (1, 1), (5, 1), (1, 7), (5, 7), (8, 4)

Write coordinates of a square with a missing point. Your partner says the missing coordinate. Repeat for a rectangle.

True or false?

7   Points on a horizontal line have the same vertical coordinate.

8   The vertical axis is perpendicular to the horizontal axis.

9   Points on the vertical axis have a first coordinate of 0.

10   Points whose second coordinate is 3 lie on a straight line parallel to the horizontal axis.

Coordinates

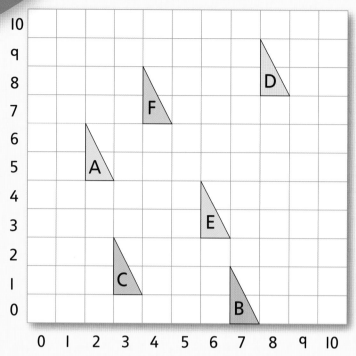

Use L for left,
R for right,
U for up,
D for down.

Describe ways of sliding from:

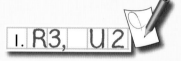
1. R3, U2

1	C to E	2	B to D	3	A to F	4	F to E
5	C to B	6	E to D	7	A to B	8	C to D
9	E to A	10	E to F	11	C to A	12	B to E

 Find a route to slide triangle A so that it visits each of the other triangles. Is it the shortest route?

A square has coordinates: (3, 3), (5, 3), (5, 5), (3, 5). Write its new coordinates when it slides:

13. (1,2),...

13 left 2, down 1

14 right 3, up 2

15 down 3, right 1

16 up 1, left 3

Polygons

1   Are these polygons – yes or no?

1. (a) Yes

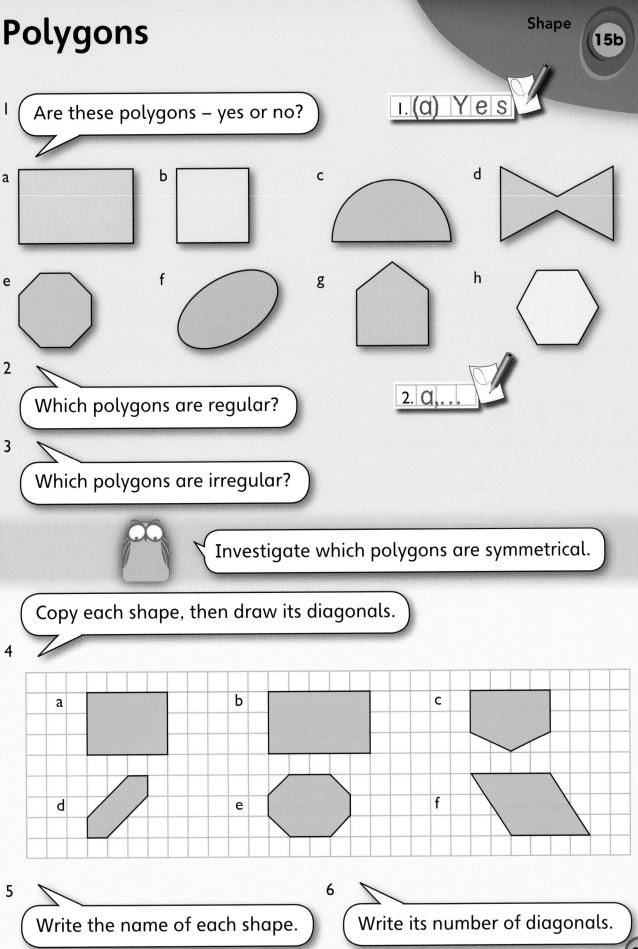

a   b   c   d

e   f   g   h

2   Which polygons are regular?

2. a, . . .

3   Which polygons are irregular?

Investigate which polygons are symmetrical.

Copy each shape, then draw its diagonals.

4

a   b   c

d   e   f

5   Write the name of each shape.

6   Write its number of diagonals.

Polygons

Write the number of sides in:

1   an isosceles triangle

2   an irregular pentagon

3   a regular octagon

4   a scalene triangle

5   Draw round the regular shapes listed in the table, then copy and complete the table.

Shape	Number of sides	Number of diagonals
quadrilateral		
pentagon		
hexagon		

Each line is a diagonal of a quadrilateral. Copy the line and draw the quadrilateral.

6    7    8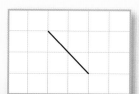

Explore

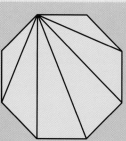

Draw round a regular octagon.

Draw all the diagonals from one vertex using a blue pencil. How many are there?

Repeat for the second vertex, using a different colour.

Keep going like this. What patterns are there?

Have you drawn all of the diagonals? How can you be sure?

Polygons

Copy each shape onto dotted paper, then draw its diagonals.

1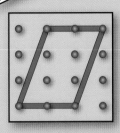

2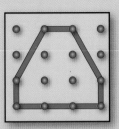

3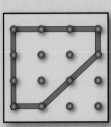

4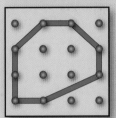

5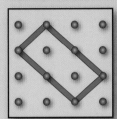

6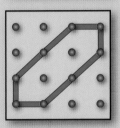

Write the name of each shape, and its number of diagonals.

 Draw a shape on a 4 × 4 grid that has only two diagonals that are both the same length. How many more shapes like this can you draw?

True or false?

7 The sides of a regular polygon are all equal.

8 A regular quadrilateral is called a square.

9 A triangle never has a diagonal.

10 All pentagons have a total of five diagonals.

11 The diagonals of a square are perpendicular to each other.

12 Regular polygons are always symmetrical.

13 A regular triangle is called an equilateral triangle.

14 A rectangle is an irregular polygon.

15 If all the diagonals of a polygon are the same length, it must be a regular polygon.

Area

Write the area of each rectangle.

1. Area = 15 cm²

1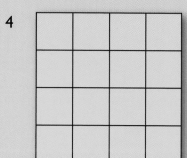

2

3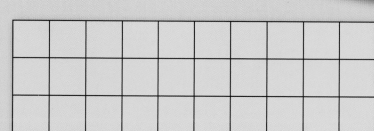

4

5

Measure the sides of these rectangles in centimetres. Find the area of each in cm².

6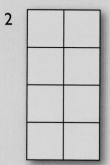

7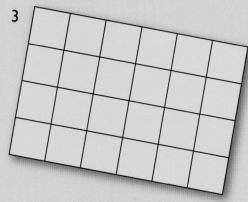

8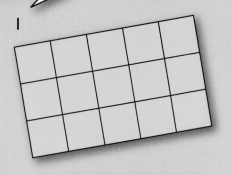

Investigate how you could find the area of a right-angled triangle.

Area

Write the area of each portrait in square centimetres.

1. $Area = 8 \times 6 = 48\,cm^2$

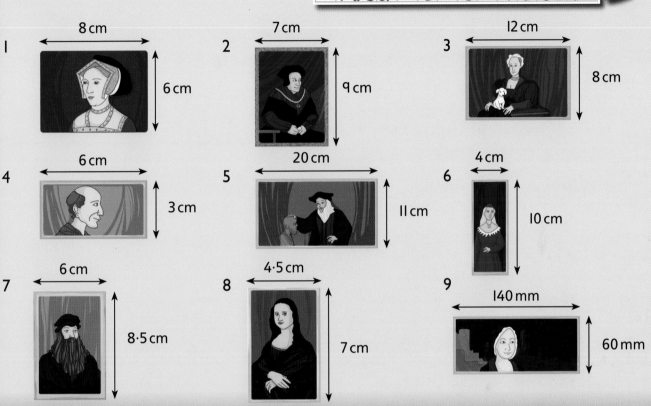

1   8 cm   6 cm

2   7 cm   9 cm

3   12 cm   8 cm

4   6 cm   3 cm

5   20 cm   11 cm

6   4 cm   10 cm

7   6 cm   8·5 cm

8   4·5 cm   7 cm

9   140 mm   60 mm

A picture has an area of 120 cm². What possible sizes could the picture be?

10   A garden has an area of 285 m², and it is 15 m wide. How long is the garden?

11   A square patio has an area of 81 m². How many centimetres long is the patio?

12   A rectangle has an area of 98 cm². Its length is double its width. How wide is it?

13   A carpet costs £4·50 per square metre. What is the cost of carpeting a room that measures 9 m by 7 m?

Large areas

What units would you use to measure the area of:

1 this textbook page   2 a postcard   3 the floor

4 your toenail   5 the playground   6 Sheffield?

Write the area of these plots of land.

7. $13 \times 40 = 520\,m^2$

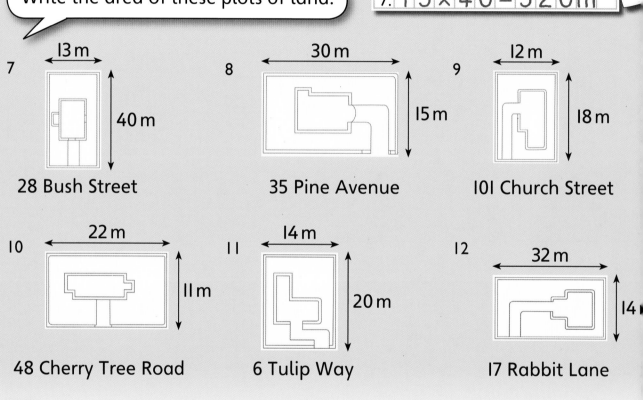

7

13 m

40 m

28 Bush Street

8

30 m

15 m

35 Pine Avenue

9

12 m

18 m

101 Church Street

10

22 m

11 m

48 Cherry Tree Road

11

14 m

20 m

6 Tulip Way

12

32 m

14

17 Rabbit Lane

Think of something that has an area you could measure in two different units, such as cm^2 or m^2. Discuss it with a partner.

 **Explore**

Investigate the area of rectangles that have one side double the length of the other. Can you find any patterns?

Small areas

Write the areas of these stamps.

1. Area = 50 × 18 = 900 mm²

1 50 mm

18 mm

2 30 mm

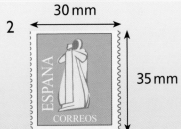

35 mm

3 43 mm

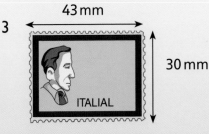

30 mm

4 1·4 cm

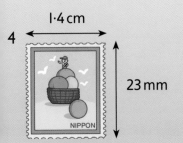

23 mm

5 2·1 cm

25 mm

6 4·2 cm

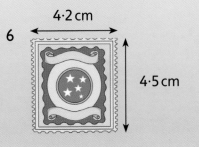

4·5 cm

🔍 Explore

Investigate how many different rectangles you can draw that have an area between 10 cm² and 20 cm².

Copy and complete.

1 m² = 10 000 cm²   1 cm² = 100 mm²

7   2 cm² = ☐ mm²   8   3 m² = ☐ cm²

9   $\frac{1}{2}$ cm² = ☐ mm²   10 $\frac{1}{4}$ m² = ☐ cm²

11   $\frac{1}{10}$ m² = ☐ cm²   12 $\frac{3}{4}$ cm² = ☐ mm²

13   $\frac{2}{5}$ cm² = ☐ mm²   14   1 m² = ☐ mm²

Perimeter

Find the perimeter of each poster.

1. $P = 24 + 40 = 64\,cm$

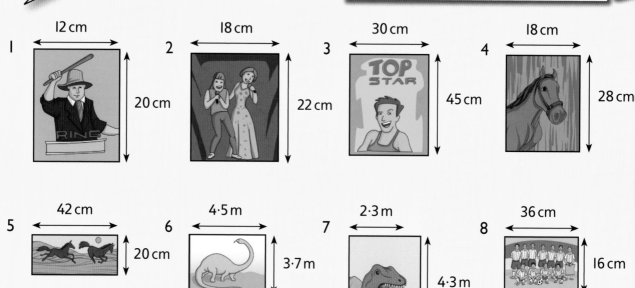

1 — 12 cm, 20 cm	2 — 18 cm, 22 cm	3 — 30 cm, 45 cm	4 — 18 cm, 28 cm
5 — 42 cm, 20 cm	6 — 4·5 m, 3·7 m	7 — 2·3 m, 4·3 m	8 — 36 cm, 16 cm

Explore

The perimeter of a rectangle is 36 cm.

Investigate what length sides the rectangle could have.

Write the perimeter of a:

9 rectangle measuring 7 cm by 6 cm

10 rectangle measuring 6·5 cm by 3·5 cm

11 square with a side of 8 cm

12 square with a side of 4·25 cm

13 square with an area of 25 cm²

Perimeter

Write the perimeter of these shapes.

1. $P = 8 + 4 = 12\,cm$

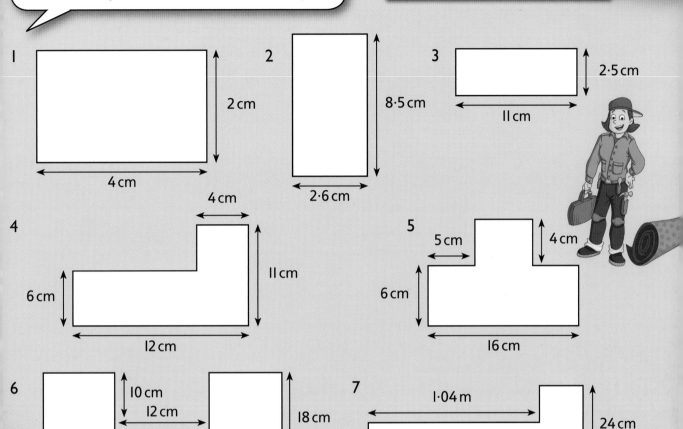

1. 2 cm, 4 cm

2. 8·5 cm, 2·6 cm

3. 2·5 cm, 11 cm

4. 4 cm, 11 cm, 6 cm, 12 cm

5. 5 cm, 4 cm, 6 cm, 16 cm

6. 10 cm, 12 cm, 18 cm, 32 cm

7. 1·04 m, 24 cm, 1·2 m

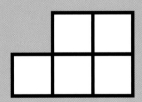 **Explore**

Use five squares of equal size.

Make different shapes by joining the squares edge to edge.

How many different shapes can you make, and what are their perimeters?

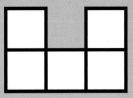

P = 10 units

P = 12 units

Perimeter

Write the perimeter of these regular polygons.

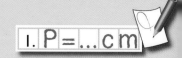

1 7 cm	2 6·5 cm	3 4·5 cm

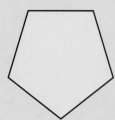  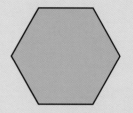

Write the length of a side of:

4 a regular octagon with a perimeter of 176 cm

5 an equilateral triangle with a perimeter of 48 mm

6 a regular decagon with a perimeter of 1·6 m

A regular polygon has a perimeter of 60 cm. What could it be?

7 A rectangular picture has an area of 48 cm², and a perimeter of 28 cm. What size is the picture?

8 A square has a perimeter of 28 cm. What is its area?

9 The rectangular lawn in a garden measures 9 m by 7 m. The lawn is surrounded by a 2 m border. What is the perimeter of the garden?

10 A regular hexagon has a perimeter that is double the perimeter of a regular pentagon. If a side of the pentagon is 6 cm, what is the length of the side of the hexagon?

Perimeter

For each polygon:
(a) estimate its perimeter
(b) measure the length of each side in cm, using decimals
(c) find its perimeter
(d) find the difference between (a) and (c)

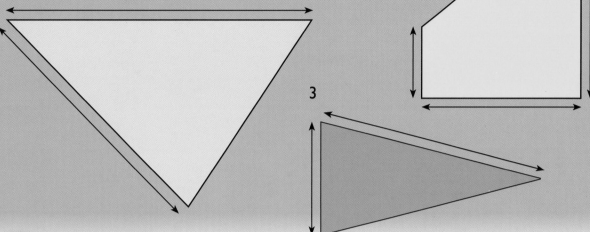

Explore

A rectangle has sides that are whole numbers in length.
Its length is double its width.

Try drawing some examples.

Is the perimeter always a multiple of 6? If so, can you explain why?

In these rectangles, A = area, P = perimeter, l = length and w = width.
Follow the instructions each time.

4   l = 6 cm, w = 4 cm. Find P.   5   l = 8 cm, w = 3 cm. Find A.

6   l = 6 cm, P = 22 cm. Find A.   7   w = 3 cm, A = 27 cm². Find l.

8   l = 8 cm, P = 40 cm. Find w.   9   A = 10 cm², w = 2 cm. Find P.

10 A = 48 cm², P = 32 cm. Find l.   11 A = 40 cm², P = 26 cm. Find w.

1 Write these units of time in order, from smallest to largest.

| hour | day | millennium | month | year | century |

| second | decade | minute | fortnight | week |

Write the units of time that are:

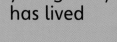
2. minute, ...

2 less than an hour

3 more than a month

4 the same as 2 weeks

5 more than a year

6 more than a minute, less than a day

7 more than a week, less than a year

8 more than a month and less than a decade

Write the units you would use to measure how long:

9 a runner takes to run a marathon (26 miles)

10 a football match takes

11 a holiday at the seaside might last

12 a large meal takes to eat

13 your granny has lived

14 a baby less than 2 years old has lived

15 it takes to climb a tree

16 your favourite television programme lasts

How many seconds does your birthday last? Work with a partner and use a calculator to find out.

Time

> Write each length of time using the smaller units.

1. $5 \times 60 = 300$ seconds

1 5 minutes (seconds)

2 2 days (hours)

3 4 weeks (days)

4 3 years (months)

5 a fortnight (days)

6 2 decades (years)

7 10 hours (minutes)

8 3 months (days)

9 9 days (hours)

10 24 hours (minutes)

11 Li Mei babysits for her younger brother for 150 minutes. She is paid £5 per hour. How much does she earn?

12 Nilesh has just had his seventh birthday. His mum says he is nearly 100 months old. Is she right?

13 Amy makes a cake that has to cook for $2\frac{1}{2}$ hours. If she takes it out 5 minutes early, how many minutes was it in the oven?

 Explore

With a partner, estimate how many hours each week you spend doing the activities in the table.

Eating	Sleeping	Reading	Watching TV	Playing	Playing sport

Copy the table and fill it in.

 Write how old you will be in 2012, 2022, 2050. Try some other dates.

Time

Write the number of days in:

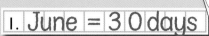
1. June = 3 0 days

1	June	2 May	3 October	4 July
5	September	6 August	7 November	8 January
9	March	10 February	11 April	12 December

Write each length of time using another unit.

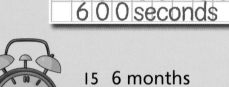
13. 1 0 × 6 0 = 6 0 0
6 0 0 seconds

13 10 minutes	14 $3\frac{1}{2}$ days	15 6 months
16 2 years	17 6 hours	18 5 minutes
19 1 month	20 1 day	21 1 fortnight
22 2 decades	23 $\frac{1}{4}$ of a year	24 5 days
25 15 minutes	26 1 century	27 24 hours

Can you turn them into another unit?

13. $\frac{1}{6}$ of an hour

Write the leap years between the year of your birth and the year when you will be 50 years old.

1. 720 minutes

> Write the intervals between:

	in minutes		in days		in months
1	7:00 am and 7:00 pm	2	31st August and 1st October	3	1 June 2001 and 1 July 2002
4	1:45 pm and 5:30 pm	5	1st May and 25th December	6	1 March 2003 and 1 September 2005
7	10:00 am and 12:35 pm	8	September 12th and January 1st	9	1 August 2005 and 1 May 2006

10 Ashanya has a holiday in Sri Lanka. It lasts 2 weeks and 3 days. How many hours is this?

11 Heather's baby is 6 weeks old today. How many hours will it be until he is 50 days old?

12 Larry is $2\frac{1}{2}$ years older than Harry. Harry is 260 weeks old. How many years old is Larry?

> Write the number of days between:

13 Christmas Day and 1st February

14 New Year's Day and 3rd March

15 the start of spring (March 21st) and the end of summer (September 21st)

16 the winter solstice (21st December) and Valentine's Day (14th February)

17 today and the end of term

18 your birthday and the end of the year

> Write the age of someone in your family in weeks.

Time

Write each time as am or pm.

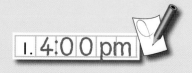 1. 4:00 pm

1	four o'clock in the afternoon	2	ten to one in the morning
3	half past six in the evening	4	twenty past midnight
5	six o'clock in the morning	6	half past ten at night
7	quarter to eight in the morning	8	twenty-five past two in the afternoon
9	five to six in the afternoon	10	quarter past three in the afternoon

Write each as a digital time, using a 24-hour clock.

11. 03:00

11   am

12   pm

13   am

14   pm

15   am

16   pm

Write some 24-hour times where the hours and the minutes are the same, e.g. 16:16. Mark each one as am or pm.

Time

Write each time using a 24-hour clock.

1. 19:05

1   five past seven pm

2   two-fifteen am

3   six forty-two pm

4   eight-thirteen am

5   quarter to seven am

6   twenty-five past eight pm

7   nine fifty-three am

8   twelve past three pm

9   half past four pm

10   five thirty-five am

True or false?

11   Ten minutes after midnight is 12:10 on a 24-hour clock.

12   Twenty to four can be 15:40 or 3:40.

13   13:13 is around lunchtime.

14   From 10:30 to 14:00 is $4\frac{1}{2}$ hours.

15   17:30 is midway between 10 am and midnight.

16   An hour later than ten to five in the morning is 05:50.

 How many palindromic digital times can you write, e.g. 15:51? How many are am times and how many are pm times?

Timetables

Place		Flight 1	Flight 2	Flight 3
London	take off	10:30	12:30	14:30
Paris	land	11:35	13:35	15:35
	take off	12:05	14:05	16:05
Amsterdam	land	13:40	15:40	17:40
	take off	14:20	16:20	18:20
Dublin	land	15:55	17:55	19:55
	take off	16:25	18:25	20:25
Edinburgh	land	17:05	19:05	21:05
	take off	17:25	19:25	21:25
London	land	18:35	20:35	22:35

Study the timetable and answer the questions.

At what times do planes take off from:
1 Dublin   2 London   3 Paris   4 Amsterdam?

At what times do planes land in:
5 Edinburgh   6 Paris   7 London   8 Dublin?

How long are these journeys:
9 Amsterdam to Dublin   10 Paris to Amsterdam

11 London to Paris   12 Dublin to Edinburgh

13 Edinburgh to London?

14 Between daytime flights, how long does a plane stop at the airport? What fraction of the day is this?

Think of four places you would like to visit. Draw up your own plane timetable.

Timetables

> Draw up a timetable to show all the following train times.

1

Dozetown
11:03
12:52
15:31
18:18

Sleepville
10:54
12:43
15:22
18:09

Snoreton
10:15
12:04
14:43
17:30

Little Boring
10:32
12:21
15:00
17:47

Snoozeford
11:26
13:15
15:54
18:41

> Write how long it takes to get from:

2 Snoreton to Little Boring

3 Little Boring to Sleepville

4 Sleepville to Dozetown

5 Dozetown to Snoozeford

6 Snoreton to Sleepville

7 Little Boring to Dozetown

8 Sleepville to Snoozeford

9 Little Boring to Snoozeford

10 How long is the train's total journey?

 **Explore**

A train goes from A to B. It takes 2 hours and 45 minutes, and stops in eight places. Devise a timetable, and calculate the time from each stop to the next.

Adding

Each judge gives the skaters three scores. What is the total?

1. $6 + 4 + 8 = 18$

Hint: Choose the order in which to add the numbers.

1 6 8 4

2 8 9 4

3 5 7 3

4 8 3 5

5 6 5 2

6 3 5 6

7 8 2 5

8 7 6 4

9 Choose four cards. Find a total. Repeat eight times.

9. $4 + 5 + 7 + 8 = 24$

Find four numbers that add to 21. They must all be different. Can you find any more?

Adding

Each child has some vouchers.
How much are they worth in total?

Hint: Choose your order.

1. £7 + £3 + £6 + £5 + £8 = £29

| | | 10 | | | | 11 | | | | | | |

1

£5 £8 £7 £6 £3

2

£8 £8 £9 £6 £4

3

£5 £8 £3 £3 £6

4

£3 £5 £5 £6 £4

5

£7 £8 £9 £3 £4

6

£6 £8 £4 £5 £7

7

£8 £6 £6 £3 £5

8

£4 £8 £7 £4 £3

Rashida has five vouchers that have a total
value of £40. What could the vouchers be?

Copy and complete.

9. 8 + 2 + 7 + 6 + 9 = 32

Hint: Choose your order.

9 7 + 8 + 9 + 6 + 2 = ☐

10 8 + 9 + 7 + 5 + 9 = ☐

11 4 + 3 + 5 + 8 + 9 = ☐

12 7 + 6 + 3 + 4 + 8 = ☐

13 6 + 5 + 8 + 8 + 4 = ☐

14 5 + 3 + 6 + 6 + 4 = ☐

15 7 + 7 + 4 + 6 + 5 = ☐

16 3 + 5 + 5 + 7 + 8 = ☐

Adding

Find each total.

1. £40 + £60 + £30 + £90 = £220
   £100   £120

1   £40 £60 £30 £90

2   £70 £80 £60 £70 £30

3   £20 £40 £60 £70 £90

4   £50 £60 £90 £30

5   £50 £40 £70 £20 £30 £50

6   £80 £90 £70 £20 £30

7   £60 £50 £40 £30

8   £20 £90 £50 £30 £30

The table shows how much each plant grew each month.
Use the table to answer the questions.

9. (a) 130 cm

9   How much did each plant grow in the first 6 months of the year?

Plant	Jan	Feb	March	April	May	June
(a) Bogsquash	60 cm	70 cm	30 cm	80 cm	20 cm	80 cm
(b) Treacleflower	70 cm	90 cm	80 cm	60 cm	50 cm	30 cm
(c) Googlygorse	40 cm	40 cm	60 cm	50 cm	70 cm	20 cm
(d) Squiffleweed	30 cm	60 cm	70 cm	80 cm	50 cm	40 cm
(e) Bumbleroot	80 cm	60 cm	50 cm	30 cm	70 cm	50 cm
(f) Bogglerot	60 cm	50 cm	80 cm	60 cm	50 cm	40 cm

10   How much did all the plants grow in each month?

If each plant grew 20 cm each month for the rest of
the year, how much will each one have grown in a year?

Adding

Khim collects the sap from his trees. How much does he collect from each tree in 1 week?

1. Tree 1 = 60 + 70 + 60 + ... + 60 = ... ml

	Monday	Tuesday	Wednesday	Thursday	Friday	Saturday	Sunday
Tree 1	60 ml	70 ml	60 ml	50 ml	60 ml	20 ml	60 ml
Tree 2	20 ml	30 ml	50 ml	60 ml	20 ml	30 ml	70 ml
Tree 3	50 ml	80 ml	60 ml	40 ml	50 ml	80 ml	20 ml
Tree 4	70 ml	70 ml	50 ml	20 ml	60 ml	50 ml	80 ml
Tree 5	90 ml	50 ml	80 ml	90 ml	70 ml	80 ml	90 ml

Which of Khim's trees gives the greatest amount of sap? The least amount? What is the difference?

Find the missing numbers.

2   30 + 60 + 40 + ☐ + 20 = 200

3   40 + 20 + ☐ + 30 + 70 = 200

4   70 + 50 + 30 + ☐ + 80 = 250

5   60 + 50 + 40 + ☐ + 50 = 280

6   30 + 20 + ☐ + 80 = 150

7   60 + 50 + ☐ + 70 + 40 + 30 = 360

Explore

How many ways can you create a bunch of six different flowers from these choices?

How much does each bunch cost?

70p   40p   80p   95p   50p   60p   90p

Adding

The child with the card total nearest 100 wins a prize. Work out each person's total. Who is the winner?

1. Sarah

3 0	+	7 0	=	1 0 0
6	+	2	=	8
3 6	+	7 2	=	1 0 8

Sarah

36 72

Jess

54 25

Jeda

61 38

Ling

44 32

Omar

64 52

Kylie

83 25

Hugh

33 56

Bilal

24 63

Samina

24 53

Jason

78 59

Halima

71 38

Alison

54 28

Copy and complete.

2.
3 0	+	4 0	=	7 0
5	+	3	=	8
3 5	+	4 3	=	7 8

2   35 + 43 = ☐

3   54 + 26 = ☐

4   37 + 21 = ☐

5   28 + 32 = ☐

6   76 + 28 = ☐

7   27 + 51 = ☐

8   82 + 16 = ☐

9   39 + 43 = ☐

10   71 + 26 = ☐

11   73 + 54 = ☐

12   85 + 78 = ☐

13   67 + 38 = ☐

☐☐ + ☐☐ = 100. Use digit cards 1–9 to find different ways of making this addition work.

Adding

Each golfer makes three putts. Write the total length.

1.	20 + 50 + 60	=	1 3 0
	5 + 4 + 3	=	...
	25 + 54 + 63	=	... cm

1

25 cm
54 cm
63 cm

2

36 cm
42 cm
28 cm

3

51 cm
64 cm
37 cm

4

19 cm
28 cm
32 cm

5   26 cm
64 cm
37 cm

6   35 cm
28 cm
47 cm

7   56 cm
48 cm
32 cm

8   63 cm
58 cm
29 cm

Copy and complete.

9.	20 + 40 + 30 + 20	=	1 1 0
	6 + 3 + 8 + 4	=	...
	26 + 43 + 38 + 24	=	...

9   26 + 43 + 38 + 24 =

10 35 + 54 + 38 + 15 =

11 19 + 63 + 28 + 36 =

12 24 + 35 + 41 + 32 =

13 22 + 38 + 53 + 45 =

14 61 + 28 + 39 + 46 =

15 17 + 46 + 28 + 62 =

16 37 + 42 + 61 + 24 =

Find ways of adding three numbers to make 101.

Adding

How much must each small rabbit grow to be the same weight as his friend?

1.
$$68 + 32 = 100$$
$$32 + 25 = 57$$
$$68 + 57 = 125g$$

1
125 g   68 g

2
111 g   72 g

3
123 g   65 g

4
134 g   69 g

5
132 g   78 g

6
126 g   74 g

7
128 g   82 g

Find the missing numbers.

8.
$$40 + 20 = 60$$
$$6 + 7 = 13$$
$$46 + 27 = 73$$
$$73 + 47 = 120$$

8   $46 + 27 + \square = 120$

9   $35 + \square + 54 = 132$

10   $\square + 28 + 46 = 94$

11   $63 + 19 + \square = 125$

12   $27 + \square + 65 = 120$

13   $42 + \square + 57 = 126$

14   $\square + 57 + 38 = 146$

15   $\square + 28 + 19 = 105$

16   $29 + 37 + \square = 112$

17   $47 + 33 + \square = 148$

Three numbers, a, b and c, are added: a + b + c = 120. The difference between a and b is twice the difference between b and c. What are a, b and c?

Adding

How much more to buy the magazine?

1. 76p + 24p = £1
   24p + 25p = 49p
   76p + 49p = £1.25

1
SOCCER
£1·25   76p

2
MOVIE MAGIC
£1·19   64p

3
POP WORLD
£1·49   EXCLUSIVE   65p

4
LIFE ON MARS
£1·32   82p

5
WILD LIFE
£1·21   59p

6
LET'S LAUGH
£1·47   74p

7
CARTOON CARTOON
78p   £1·38

Find the missing numbers.

8   $163 + \boxed{} = 241$

9   $154 + \boxed{} = 225$

10   $175 + \boxed{} = 253$

11   $182 + \boxed{} = 248$

12   $147 + \boxed{} = 237$

13   $158 + \boxed{} = 261$

14   $172 + \boxed{} = 259$

15   $168 + \boxed{} = 282$

16   $138 + \boxed{} = 264$

Write some questions like this where the answer is 276. Give them to your friend to complete.

Use the fact that 346 − 171 = 175 to answer these:

17   $171 + 175 = \boxed{}$

18   $346 - 175 = \boxed{}$

19   $17·1 + 17·5 = \boxed{}$

20   $3·46 - 1·71 = \boxed{}$

21   $1710 + 1750 = \boxed{}$

22   $150 + 346 - 171 = \boxed{}$

Adding

Copy and complete.

1. $27 + 40 = 67$
   $27 + 39 = 66$

1   $27 + 39 = \boxed{}$ 2 $35 + 29 = \boxed{}$ 3 $46 + 29 = \boxed{}$

4   $37 + 49 = \boxed{}$ 5 $42 + 59 = \boxed{}$ 6 $23 + 39 = \boxed{}$

7   $35 + 49 = \boxed{}$ 8 $45 + 29 = \boxed{}$ 9 $52 + 39 = \boxed{}$

Work out the total distance.

10
350 km, then 299 km

11
260 km, then 599 km

12
470 km, then 399 km

13
320 km, then 498 km

14
452 km, then 302 km

15
638 km, then 201 km

16
546 km, then 298 km

17
263 km, then 399 km

18
486 km, then 199 km

Double the distances for each place.

 A quick way of adding 199 is to add 200, then take away 1. Talk with a partner about quick ways of adding 149 and 1·9.

Adding

Each plane makes two flights. Find the total distance.

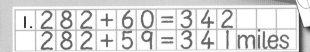

1. $282 + 60 = 342$
   $282 + 59 = 341$ miles

1   282 miles, then 59 miles

2   364 miles, then 49 miles

3   342 miles, then 189 miles

4   580 miles, then 149 miles

5   246 miles, then 69 miles

6   352 miles, then 89 miles

7   371 miles, then 79 miles

8   3006 miles, then 368 miles

9   2004 miles, then 189 miles

10   3452 miles, then 1997 miles

Copy and complete.

11. $1008 + 160 = 1168$
    $1008 + 159 = 1167$

11   $1008 + 159 = \square$

12   $472 + 198 = \square$

13   $2612 + 1997 = \square$

14   $584 + 299 = \square$

15   $3005 + 189 = \square$

16   $4361 + 1998 = \square$

17   $493 + 399 = \square$

18   $5006 + 298 = \square$

19   $5462 + 2999 = \square$

Add 9, 19, 29... up to 99. Guess first, then work out the total.

Adding

 car hire £128

 hotel £115

 ferry crossing £126

 cruise £423

 flight £212

 cottage £324

 flat £158

 tent £294

 caravan £152

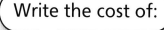 chalet £236

```
1. 200 + 100 = 300
    90 +  20 = 110
     4 +     8 =  12
   294 + 128 = 422
```

Write the cost of:

1   tent and car hire

2   tent and ferry

3   ferry and hotel

4   cruise and flight

5   car hire and chalet

6   hotel and flat

7   flight and cottage

8   ferry and cottage

9   chalet and caravan

 You have £2000 to spend for a family holiday. Which of these could you choose?

10   Liz cycles 154 km in her first week and 228 km in the second. How much further until she reaches 410 km?

11   A rucksack weighs 350 g. Jamal adds a jacket weighing 280 g and boots weighing 490 g. What is the total weight?

Copy and complete.

12   $246 + 384 = \square$

13   $346 + 238 + 34 = \square$

14   $653 + 268 = \square$

15   $467 + 429 = \square$

16   $689 + 573 = \square$

17   $576 + 739 + 56 = \square$

Adding

True or false?

1   When adding five numbers, if the units digits are all the same, the total ends in 5.

2   Three different numbers are added. The total is over 1800. All three numbers must be 3-digit numbers.

3   Adding four 3-digit numbers less than 500 cannot give a total over 2000.

4   It is possible to add another number to the sum of 373 and 737 so that the total has four identical digits.

5   The total of four 2-digit numbers, where all of the digits are odd, must be an odd number.

6   Choose three cards to make six different totals close to 900.

246   361   345   182   428   287

Choose four cards to make three different totals between 1000 and 1200.

Add two palindromic 3-digit numbers, such as 242 and 353. Is the answer a palindrome? Try some more.

Adding

How much more to make the next metre of pipe?

I. 1·3 + 0·7 = 2m

1 1·3 m

2 2·8 m

3 4·5 m

4 3·6 m

5 5·6 m

6 2·4 m

7 6·3 m

8 4·9 m

9 5·2 m

10 3·2 m

11 1·8 m

12 7·6 m

$\square \cdot \square + \square \cdot \square = 10$. Use digit cards 1–9.
How many ways can you find to complete this addition?

13 Choose a pair of railings to make 10 metres. Repeat five times.

5·4 m

7·3 m

6·8 m

1·8 m

2·7 m

3·2 m

4·6 m

5·2 m

4·8 m

8·2 m

Copy and complete.

14 4·6 + 0·7 = $\square$

15 3·8 + 0·5 = $\square$

16 2·7 + 0·6 = $\square$

17 5·5 + 0·8 = $\square$

18 6·3 + 0·6 = $\square$

19 3·5 + 0·8 = $\square$

Adding

How much more to have the next kilogram?

1. $3.6 + 0.4 = 4\,kg$

1	3·6 kg	2	2·8 kg	3	5·4 kg	4	6·2 kg
5	4·3 kg	6	6·7 kg	7	3·1 kg	8	5·9 kg

Add each pair.

9. $1.2 + 1.7 = 2.9\,kg$

9 1·2 kg + 1·7 kg   10 2·3 kg + 4·6 kg   11 1·6 kg + 2·8 kg

12 2·8 kg + 3·7 kg   13 1·8 kg + 1·5 kg   14 2·7 kg + 1·9 kg

15 Hervé has run 3·2 km. He reaches his friends in another 4·9 km. Then he runs home again! How far does he run?

16 Hayley cuts four pieces of rope: 1·2 m, 2·4 m, 1·8 m and 1·7 m. She ties them all together to make one long rope. The knots use 1·0 m of rope altogether. How long is her rope in the end?

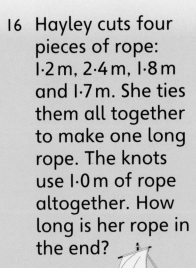

17 Mrs Barker has four dogs who weigh 7·7 kg, 7·8 kg, 8·6 kg and 8·3 kg. How much do they weigh altogether? Find the average weight by halving the total, then halving it again.

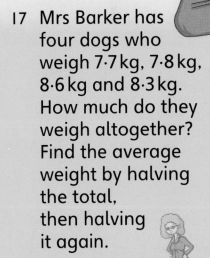

Copy and complete.

18.
2	+3	=5
0·4	+0·8	=1·2
2·4	+3·8	=6·2

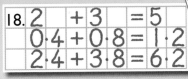

18 $2.4 + 3.8 =$ ☐   19 $3.7 + 2.4 =$ ☐   20 $6.4 + 2.8 =$ ☐

21 $5.3 + 2.6 =$ ☐   22 $3.6 + 5.5 =$ ☐   23 $2.5 + 2.7 =$ ☐

24 $4.8 + 3.6 =$ ☐   25 $2.8 + 3.9 =$ ☐   26 $7.6 + 1.5 =$ ☐

Adding

Choose three teapots. How much tea can they take? Repeat 10 times.

1

1. (a)	+	(b)	+	(c)	=		
		1	+	2	=		3
0·3	+	0·8	+	0·2	=		1·3
1·3	+	0·8	+	2·2	=	4·	3 l

a 0·8 l

b 1·3 l

c 2·2 l

d 0·7 l

e 0·6 l

f 1·1 l

g 1·5 l

h 0·9 l

i 1·6 l

Find three teapots whose total capacity is close to 4 litres. How close can you get?

Copy and complete.

2.		4	+	3	+	2	=		9
	0·5	+	0·2	+	0·6	=		1·	3
	4·5	+	3·2	+	2·6	=	10·	3

2   4·5 + 3·2 + 2·6 =

3   3·8 + 1·3 + 2·7 =

4   3·4 + 2·3 + 1·8 =

5   2·1 + 5·8 + 3·4 =

6   6·8 − 2·3 =

7   3·6 + 2·7 + 1·6 =

8   8·4 − 3·2 =

9   2·9 + 3·4 + 1·2 =

10   3·5 + 1·6 + 2·5 =

11   5·8 − 3·6 =

12   2·4 + 3·9 + 1·5 =

13   7·8 − 3·4 =

Adding

How much altogether?

1 £1·45 67p

2  £1·36 £1·27

3  £1·63 89p

4 £1·38 £1·52

5 £1·67 74p

6  £1·43 £1·29

How much is left?

7 spends £7·80 £3·50

8 spends £8·60 £5·30

9 spends £9·80 £6·30

10 spends £6·90 £4·40

11 spends £7·70 £3·40

12 spends £5·80 £2·20

Copy and complete.

13 £4·85 + £1·60 = ☐

14 £3·72 + £2·50 = ☐

15 £4·79 + £3·67 = ☐

🔍 Explore

Each parcel has to have an exact number of pounds in stamps. Each must have three stamps.

| £1·17 | £1·28 | £2·72 | 36p | £1·64 | £2·53 | 56p |

| £1·81 | 64p | 47p | £4 | £2·91 | £1·36 |

Find combinations that will work.

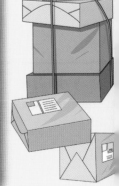

Multiples

Continue each list up to the twelfth multiple.

1. 3, 6, 9, 12, 15, …

| 1 | 3, 6, 9, 12, … | 2 | 5, 10, 15, 20, … | 3 | 8, 16, 24, … |

4 6, 12, 18, 24, …   5 9, 18, 27, …   6 7, 14, 21, 28, …

7 The highlighted numbers are multiples of 3. Describe five patterns that you can see.

1	2	3	4	5	6	7	8	9	10
11	12	13	14	15	16	17	18	19	20
21	22	23	24	25	26	27	28	29	30
31	32	33	34	35	36	37	38	39	40
41	42	43	44	45	46	47	48	49	50
51	52	53	54	55	56	57	58	59	60
61	62	63	64	65	66	67	68	69	70
71	72	73	74	75	76	77	78	79	80
81	82	83	84	85	86	87	88	89	90
91	92	93	94	95	96	97	98	99	100

8 Copy this grid. Colour the multiples of 3. Describe the patterns.

Use a different colour for multiples of:

9 5   10 4   11 7

1	2	3	4	5	6
7	8	9	10	11	12
13	14	15	16	17	18
19	20	21	22	23	24
25	26	27	28	29	30
31	32	33	34	35	36

Which size grids give column patterns for which multiples? (For example, a 6 x 6 grid gives column patterns for multiples of 2, 3 and 6.)

Multiples

Copy the Venn diagram. Make it large!
Write numbers 1–30 in the correct places.

1

multiples of 2		multiples of 3

Write three more numbers in each coloured region.

2. Green 16, ...

2

multiples of 2	multiples of 5

12

15

30

14

11

7

3

multiples of 3	multiples of 4

27

16

24

9

13

5

4

multiples of 4	multiples of 5

100

30

28

27

13

5

multiples of 3	multiples of 5

9

45

5

16

8

Write the first three numbers that are common multiples of:

6 3 and 5   **7** 4 and 3   **8** 4 and 5   **9** 5 and 6

Write a number that is not a multiple of 2, 3, or 4.
Can you write some more?

Multiples

The grid shows that the common multiples of 3 and 5 are 15, 30. They can be extended to 15, 30, 45, 60, 75…

Use the grid to help you write the first five common multiples of:

1	2	3	4	5	6	7	8	9	10
2	4	6	8	10	12	14	16	18	20
3	6	9	12	15	18	21	24	27	30
4	8	12	16	20	24	28	32	36	40
5	10	15	20	25	30	35	40	45	50
6	12	18	24	30	36	42	48	54	60
7	14	21	28	35	42	49	56	63	70
8	16	24	32	40	48	56	64	72	80
9	18	27	36	45	54	63	72	81	90
10	20	30	40	50	60	70	80	90	100

1   2 and 3   2   3 and 4   3   4 and 6

4   2 and 7   5   3 and 6   6   4 and 9

I am a number. Who am I?

7   I am a multiple of 3 and a multiple of 5. I am between 40 and 50.

8   I am a common multiple of 5 and 6. I have 2 digits. I am more than 70.

9   I am the smallest common multiple of 2, 3 and 7.

10   I am a multiple of 3 and not a multiple of 2. I am between 10 and 20.

11   I am a common multiple of 3, 4 and 5. I am between 100 and 150.

12   I am a common multiple of 3 and 7. My digits have a total of 9.

 Write your own 'Who am I?' question using common multiples. Give it to your friend to answer.

Multiples

| 24 | 48 | 100 | 64 | 42 | 40 | 28 | 90 |

| 32 | 15 | 35 | 65 | 70 | 45 | 75 | 80 |

Which of these numbers are multiples of:

1. 24, 32, ...

1 4   2 5   3 6   4 3   5 7   6 8?

Which are common multiples of:

7 3 and 4   8 2 and 3   9 4 and 6

10 5 and 4   11 3 and 5   12 5 and 6

True or false?

13 Common multiples of 3 and 4 are multiples of 12.

14 120 is a common multiple of 4 and 5.

15 Multiples of 7 are sometimes multiples of 3.

16 There are three common multiples of 5 and 6 less than 100.

17 24 is the smallest common multiple of 3 and 4.

18 There are exactly four common multiples of 2, 3, and 4 less than 100.

Explore

Use only multiples of numbers 1–12.

Investigate which numbers between 20 and 40 can be written as
(a) a multiple
(b) a common multiple of two numbers.

21 is a multiple of 7.

21 is a common multiple of 3 and 7.

20b Divisibility

Divisibility

The bank has bags of coins of the same type. Can the bags contain 10p coins – yes or no?

1. Yes ✓

1 70p 2 85p 3 90p 4 64p

5 96p 6 £3·20 7 £4·50 8 £1·75

9 £2·33 10 £3·15 11 £4·28 12 £5·36

 Can they be 2p coins? Can they be 5p coins?

 In the bags that could be 5p coins, how many coins are there?

Write five amounts that could be bags of:

 13. 10p, ...

13 2p coins or 5p coins   14 5p coins or 10p coins   15 20p coins

True or false?

16 If a number is divisible by 5, then it is also divisible by 10.

17 A number is not divisible by 4 if, when it is halved, the answer is odd.

18 If a number is divisible by 4, it is also divisible by 2.

19 800 is divisible by 2, 4, 5, 10 and 100.

Divisibility

The animals are going to the wildlife park. Can they be paired exactly in 2s – yes or no?

1. No

1 47 giraffes	2 56 horses	3 84 zebras
4 138 lions	5 249 tigers	6 54 elephants
7 427 llamas	8 109 monkeys	9 386 emus
10 245 kangaroos	11 1008 buffalo	12 478 snakes
13 97 rhinos	14 164 hippos	15 300 ostriches

For each set of animals that can be paired in 2s, write how many pairs. Can they be grouped exactly in 4s?

Write three numbers of animals that can be grouped in:

16. 6, ...

16 2s, but not in 4s

17 5s, but not in 10s

18 5s, but not in 2s

19 4s, but not in 10s

20 Write three numbers of animals that cannot be grouped in 2s, 4s, 5s or 10s.

Explore

Investigate how many numbers between 1 and 100 are divisible by 2.

How many are divisible by 4? By 5?

How many are divisible by each of 2, 4 and 5?

Divisibility

Leap years are divisible by 4. Which of these are leap years?

1

2008	1942	866	4028	1275
1394	46	1582		1943
1994	1708	2024		2070

Investigate the number of leap years in a decade, a century, a millennium.

Copy and complete this table.

2

Number	Divisible by:			
	2	5	10	4
76	✓	✗	✗	✓
85				
142				
2136				
3024				
8005				
790				
106				

Explore

A test for divisibility by 4 is to halve the number and see if the result is an even number.

Can you create a similar test for divisibility by 8? Show how, using numbers that are and are not divisible by 8.